ENGLISH COSTUME

I.—EARLY ENGLISH

ENGLISH COSTUME

BY

DION CLAYTON CALTHROP

ILLUSTRATED WITH FULL-PAGE PLATES IN
COLOUR AND MANY DIAGRAMS IN THE TEXT

EACH SECTION PRICE **7s. 6d.** NET
(POST FREE **7s. 11d.**)

I. EARLY ENGLISH
II. MIDDLE AGES
III. TUDOR AND STUART
IV. GEORGIAN

Published by
A. & C. BLACK . SOHO SQUARE . LONDON . W.

AGENTS

AMERICA . . THE MACMILLAN COMPANY
64 & 66 FIFTH AVENUE, NEW YORK

CANADA . . THE MACMILLAN COMPANY OF CANADA, LTD.
27 RICHMOND STREET, TORONTO

INDIA . . . MACMILLAN & COMPANY, LTD.
12 BANK STREET, BOMBAY
7 NEW CHINA BAZAAR STREET, CALCUTTA

A CHILD OF THE TIME OF HENRY I.

IT is only in quite recent years that there have been
quite distinct dresses for children, fashions indeed
which began with the ideas for the improvement in
hygiene. For many centuries children were dressed,
with slight modifications, after the manner of their
parents, looking like little men and women, until in
the end they arrived at the grotesque infants of
Hogarth's day, powdered and patched, with little
stiff skirted suits and stiff brocade gowns, with little
swords and little fans and, no doubt, many pretty
airs and graces.

One thing I have never seen until the early six-
teenth century, and that is girls wearing any of
the massive headgear of their parents; in all other
particulars they were the same.

ENGLISH COSTUME

BY

DION CLAYTON CALTHROP

I.

EARLY ENGLISH

LONDON
ADAM AND CHARLES BLACK
1906

Contents

v

CONTENTS

RICHARD THE FIRST

JOHN

HENRY THE THIRD

List of Illustrations

vii

INTRODUCTION

THE world, if we choose to see it so, is a compli-
cated picture of people dressing and undressing.
The history of the world is composed of the chat
of a little band of tailors seated cross-legged on
their boards; they gossip across the centuries,
feeling, as they should, very busy and important.
Someone made the coat of many colours for Joseph,
another cut into material for Elijah's mantle.

Baldwin, from his stall on the site of the great
battle, has only to stretch his neck round to nod
to the tailor who made the toga for Julius Cæsar;
has only to lean forward to smile to Pasquino, the
wittiest of tailors.

John Pepys, the tailor, gossips with his neigh-
bour who cut that jackanapes coat with silver
buttons so proudly worn by Samuel Pepys, his
son. Mr. Schweitzer, who cut Beau Brummell's
coat, talks to Mr. Meyer, who shaped his panta-

loons. Our world is full of the sound of scissors, the clipping of which, with the gossiping tongues, drown the grander voices of history.

As you will see, I have devoted myself entirely to civil costume—that is, the clothes a man or a woman would wear from choice, and not by reason of an appointment to some ecclesiastical post, or to a military calling, or to the Bar, or the Bench. Such clothes are but symbols of their trades and professions, and have been dealt with by persons who specialize in those professions.

I have taken the date of the Conquest as my starting-point, and from that date—a very simple period of clothes—I have followed the changes of the garments reign by reign, fold by fold, button by button, until we arrive quite smoothly at Beau Brummell, the inventor of modern clothes, the prophet of cleanliness.

I have taken considerable pains to trace the influence of one garment upon its successor, to reduce the wardrobe for each reign down to its simplest cuts and folds, so that the reader may follow quite easily the passage of the coat from its birth to its ripe age, and by this means may not only know the clothes of one time, but the reasons for those garments. To the best of my knowledge, such a thing has never been done before; most works on dress try to include the world from Adam to Charles Dickens, lump a century into a page, and dismiss the ancient Egyptians in a couple of colour plates.

So many young gentlemen have blown away their patrimony on feathers and tobacco that it is necessary for us to confine ourselves to certain gentlemen and ladies in our own country. A knowledge of history is essential to the study of mankind, and a knowledge of history is never perfect without a knowledge of the clothes with which to dress it.

A man, in a sense, belongs to his clothes; they are so much a part of him that, to take him seriously, one must know how he walked about, in what habit, with what air.

I am compelled to speak strongly of my own work because I believe in it, and I feel that the series of paintings in these volumes are really a valuable addition to English history. To be modest is often to be excessively vain, and, having made

And what are we doing to help modern history —the picture of our own times—that it may look beautiful in the ages to come? I cannot answer you that.

Some chapters of this work have appeared in the *Connoisseur*, and I have to thankthe editor for his courtesy in allowing me to reproduce them.

I must also thank Mr. Pownall for his help in the early stages of my labours.

One thing more I must add: I do not wish this book to go forth and be received with that frigid politeness which usually welcomes a history to the shelves of the bookcase, there to remain unread. The book is intended to be read, and is not wrapped up in grandiose phrases and a great wind about nothing; I would wish to be thought more friendly than the antiquarian and more truthful than the historian, and so have endeavoured to show, in addition to the body of the clothes, some little of their soul.

DION CLAYTON CALTHROP.

St. Valentine's Day, 1906.

WILLIAM THE FIRST

Reigned twenty-one years : 1066—1087.
Born 1027.   Married, 1053, Matilda of Flanders.

THE MEN

WHY France should always give the lead in the matter of dress is a nice point in sartorial morality — a morality which holds that it takes nine tailors to make a man and but one milliner to break him, a code, in fact, with which this book will often have to deal.

Sartorially, then, we commence with the 14th of October, 1066, upon which day, fatal to the fashions of the country, the flag of King Harold, sumptuously woven and embroidered in gold, bearing the figure of a man fighting, studded with precious stones, was captured.

William, of Norse blood and pirate traditions, landed in England, and brought with him bloodshed, devastation, new laws, new customs, and new fashions.

Principal among these last was the method of shaving the hair at the back of the head, which fashion speedily died out by reason of the parlous times and the haste of war, besides the utter absurdity of the idea. Fashion, however, has no sense of the ridiculous, and soon replaced the one folly by some other extravagance.

William I. found the Saxons very plainly dressed, and he did little to alter the masculine mode.

He found the Saxon ladies to be as excellent at embroidery as were their Norman sisters, and in such times the spindle side was content to sit patiently at home weaving while the men were abroad ravaging the country.

William was not of the stuff of dandies. No man could draw his bow; he helped with his own hands to clear the snowdrift on the march to Chester. Stark and fierce he was, loving the

A MAN OF THE TIME OF WILLIAM I.
(1066—1087)

CLOAK buckled at the shoulder. Leather thongs crossed on his legs. Shoes of leather. Tunic fitting to his body like a jersey.

solitudes of the woods and the sight of hart and hind.

When some kind of order was restored in England, many of the Saxons who had fled the country and gone to Constantinople came back, bringing with them the Oriental idea of dress. The Jews came with Eastern merchandise into England, and brought rich-coloured stuffs, and as these spread through the country by slow degrees, there came a gradual change in colour and material, and finer stuffs replaced the old homespun garments.

The Jews were at this time very eminent as silk manufacturers and makers of purple cloth. The Britons had been very famous for their dyed woollen stuffs. Boadicea is said to have worn a tunic of chequered stuff, which was in all probability rather of the nature of Scotch plaids.

The tunics worn by the men of this time were, roughly speaking, of two kinds : those that fitted close to the body, and those that hung loose, being gathered into the waist by a band. The close-fitting tunic was in the form of a knitted jersey, with skirts reaching to the knee ; it was open on either side to the hips, and fell from the hips in loose folds. The neck was slit open four or five

inches, and had an edging of embroidery, and the
sleeves were wide, and reached just below the

elbows. These also had an
edging of embroidery, or a
band different in colour to
the rest of the tunic.

The other form of tunic
was made exactly in shape
like the modern shirt, except
that the neck opening was
smaller. It was loose and
easy, with wide sleeves to the
elbow, and was gathered in
at the waist by a band of stuff
or leather.

The skirts of the tunics were cut square or
V-shaped in front and behind. There were also
tunics similar in shape to either of those mentioned,
except that the skirts were very short, and were
tucked into wide, short breeches which reached to
the knee, or into the trousers which men wore.

Under this tunic was a plain shirt, loosely fitting,
the sleeves tight and wrinkled over the wrist, the
neck showing above the opening of the tunic.
This shirt was generally white, and the opening

at the neck was sometimes stitched with coloured or black wool.

Upon the legs they wore neat-fitting drawers of wool or cloth, dyed or of natural colour, or loose trousers of the same materials, sometimes worn loose, but more generally bound round just above the knee and at the ankle.

They wore woollen socks, and for footgear they wore shoes of skin and leather, and boots of soft leather shaped naturally to the foot and strapped or buckled across the instep. The tops of the boots were sometimes ornamented with coloured bands.

The cloak worn was semicircular in shape, with or without a small semicircle cut out at the neck. It was fastened over the right shoulder or in the centre by means of a large round or square brooch, or it was held in place by means of a metal ring or a stuff loop through which the cloak was pushed; or it was tied by two cords sewn on to the right side of the cloak, which cords took a bunch of the stuff into a knot and so held it, the ends of the cords having tags of metal or plain ornaments.

One may see the very same make and fashion of tunic as the Normans wore under their armour being worn to-day by the Dervishes in Lower Egypt —a coarse wool tunic, well padded, made in the

form of tunic and short drawers in one piece, the wide sleeves reaching just below the elbow.

The hats and caps of these men were of the most simple form—plain round-topped skull-caps, flat caps close to the head without a brim, and a hat with a peak like the helmet.

Hoods, of course, were worn during the winter, made very close to the head, and they were also worn under the helmets.

Thus in such a guise may we picture the Norman lord at home, eating his meat with his fingers, his feet in loose skin shoes tied with thongs, his legs in loose trousers bound with crossed garters, his tunic open at the neck showing the white edge of his shirt, his face clean-shaven, and his hair neatly cropped.

THE WOMEN

Nothing could be plainer or more homely than the dress of a Norman lady. Her loose gown was made with ample skirts reaching well on to the ground, and it was gathered in at the waist by a belt of wool, cloth, silk, or cloth of gold web.

The gown fitted easily across the shoulders, but fell from there in loose folds. The neck opening was cut as the man's, about five inches down the front, and the border ornamented with some fine needlework, as also were the borders of the wide sleeves, which came just below the elbows.

Often the gown was made short, so that when it was girded up the border of it fell only to the knees, and showed the long chemise below.

The girdle was, perhaps, the richest portion of their attire, and was sometimes of silk diapered with gold thread, but such a girdle would be very costly. More often it would be plain wool, and be tied simply round the waist with short ends, which did not show.

The chemise was a plain white garment, with tight sleeves which wrinkled at the wrists; that is to say, they were really too long for the arm, and so were caught in small folds at the wrist.

The gown, opening at the neck in the same way as did the men's tunics, showed the white of the

chemise, the opening being held together sometimes by a brooch.

Towards the end of the reign the upper part of the gown—that is, from the neck to the waist—was worn close and fitted more closely to the figure, but not over-tightly— much as a tight jersey would fit.

Over all was a cloak of the semicircular shape, very voluminous—about three feet in diameter—which was brooched in the centre or on the shoulder.

On the head, where the hair was closely coiled with a few curls at the forehead, a wimple was worn, which was wound about the head and thrown

A WOMAN OF THE TIME OF WILLIAM I.
(1066—1087)

A TWIST of wool holds the gown at the waist. Under
the gown the chemise shows. The neck of the gown
is embroidered.

over the shoulder, not allowing the hair to show. These wimples were sometimes very broad, and were almost like a mantle, so that they fell over the shoulders below the breast.

Tied round the wimple they sometimes had a snood, or band of silk.

The shoes were like those worn by the men.

These ladies were all housewives, cooking, preparing simples, doing embroidery and weaving. They were their own milliners and dressmakers, and generally made their husbands' clothes, although some garments might be made by the town tailors; but, as a rule, they weaved, cut, sewed, and fitted for their families, and then, after the garments were finished to satisfaction, they would begin upon strips of embroidery to decorate them.

In such occupation we may picture them, and imagine them sitting by the windows with their ladies, busily sewing, looking up from their work to see hedged fields in lambing-time, while shepherds in rough sheepskin clothes drove the sheep into a neat enclosure, and saw to it that they lay on warm straw against the cold February night.

WILLIAM THE SECOND

Reigned thirteen years: 1087—1100.
Born *c.* 1060.

THE MEN

ABOUT this time there came to England a Norman, who settled near by the Abbey of Battle — Baldwin the Tailor by name, whom one might call the father of English tailoring.

Baldwin the Tailor sat contentedly cross - legged on his bench and plied his needle and thread, and snipped, and cut, and sewed, watching the birds pick worms and insects from the turf of the battleground.

10

A MAN OF THE TIME OF WILLIAM II.
(1087—1100)

SHOWS the wide drawers with an embroidered hem.
Under them can be seen the long woollen drawers
bound with leather thongs.

England is getting a little more settled.

The reign opens picturesquely enough with William Rufus hastening to England with his father's ring, and ends with the tragedy of the New Forest and a blood-stained tunic.

Clothes begin to play an important part. Rich fur-lined cloaks and gowns trail on the ground, and sweep the daisies so lately pressed by mailed feet and sopped with blood where the Saxons fell.

Times have changed since Baldwin was at the coronation at Westminster on Christmas Day twenty years ago. Flemish weavers and farmers arrive from overseas, and are established by William II. in the North to teach the people pacific arts,

The Cloak pushed through a Ring.

causing in time astream of Flemish merchandise to flow into the country, chiefly of rich fabrics and fine cloths.

2—2

The men adopt longer tunics, made after the same pattern as before—split up either side and loose in the sleeve—but in many cases the skirts reach to the ground in heavy folds, and the sleeves hang over the hands by quite a yard.

The necks of these tunics are ornamented as before, with coloured bands or stiff embroidery.

The cuffs have the embroidery both inside and out, so that when the long sleeve is turned back over the hand the embroidery will show.

The fashion in cloaks is still the same—of a semicircular pattern.

The shoes are the same as in the previous reign—that is, of the shape of the foot, except in rare cases of dandyism, when the shoes were made with long, narrow toes, and these, being stuffed with moss or wool, were so stiffened and curled up at the ends that they presented what was supposed to be a delightfully extravagant appearance.

They wore a sort of ankle garter of soft leather or cloth, which came over the top of the boot and just above the ankle.

The hair, beard, and moustaches were worn long and carefully combed—in fact, the length of the beard caused the priests to rail at them under such terms as 'filthy goats.' But they had hardly the right to censorship, since they themselves had to be severely reprimanded by their Bishops for their extravagance in dress.

Many gentlemen, and especially the Welsh, wore long loose trousers as far as the ankle, leaving these garments free from any cross gartering. These were secured about the waist by a girdle of stuff or leather.

The ultra - fashion-able dress was an elongation of every part of the simple dress of the previous reign. Given these few details, it is easy for anyone who wishes to go further to do so, in which case he must keep to the main out-line very carefully; but as to the actual length of sleeve or shoe, or the very measurements of a cloak, they varied with the individual folly of the owner. So a man might have long sleeves and a short tunic, or a tunic which trailed upon the ground, the sleeves of which reached only to the elbow.

I have noticed that it is the general custom of writers upon the dress of this early time to dwell lovingly upon the colours of the various parts of the dress as they were painted in the illuminated manuscripts. This is a foolish waste of time, insomuch as the colours were made the means of displays of pure design on the part of the very early illuminators ; and if one were to go upon such evidence as this, by the exactness of such drawings alone, then every Norman had a face the colour of which nearly resembled wet biscuit, and hair picked out in brown lines round each wave and curl.

These woollen clothes—cap, tunic, semicircular cloak, and leg coverings — have all been actually found in the tomb of a Briton of the Bronze Age. So little did the clothes alter in shape, that the early Briton and the late Norman were dressed nearly exactly alike.

When the tomb of William II. was opened in 1868, it was found, as had been suspected, that the grave had been opened and looted of what valuables it might have contained ; but there were found among the dust which filled the bottom of the tomb fragments of red cloth, of gold cloth, a turquoise, a serpent's head in ivory, and a wooden spear shaft, perhaps the very spear that William carried on that fatal day in the New Forest.

Also with the dust and bones of the dead King some nutshells were discovered, and examination showed that mice had been able to get into the tomb. So, if you please, you may hit upon a pretty moral.

THE WOMEN

And so the lady began to lace. . . .

A moralist, a denouncer of the fair sex, a satirist, would have his fling at this. What thundering epithets and avalanche of words should burst out at such a momentous point in English history !

However, the lady pleased herself.

Not that the lacing was very tight, but it commenced the habit, and the habit begat the harm, and the thing grew until it arrived finally at that buckram, square-built, cardboard-and-tissue figure which titters and totters through the Elizabethan era.

Our male eyes, trained from infancy upwards to avoid gazing into certain shop windows, nevertheless retain a vivid impression of an awesome affair therein, which we understood by hints and signs confined our mothers' figures in its deadly grip.

That the lady did not lace herself overtight is proved by the many informations we have of her household duties ; that she laced tight enough for unkind comment is shown by the fact that some old monk pictured the devil in a neat-laced gown.

It was, at any rate, a distinct departure from the loosely-clothed lady of 1066 towards the neater figure of 1135.

The lacing was more to draw the wrinkles of the close-woven bodice of the gown smooth than to form a false waist and accentuated hips, the beauty of which malformation I must leave to the writers in ladies' journals and the condemnation to health faddists.

However, the lacing was not the only matter of note. A change was coming over all feminine apparel—a change towards richness, which made itself felt in this reign more in the fabric than in the actual make of the garment.

The gown was open at the neck in the usual

A WOMAN OF THE TIME OF WILLIAM II.
(1087—1100)

THIS shows the gown, which is laced behind, fitting more closely to the figure. The sleeves are wider above the wrist.

manner, was full in the skirt and longer than
heretofore, was laced at the back, and was loose
in the sleeve.

The sleeve as worn by the men—that is, the over-
long sleeve hanging down over the hand—was also
worn by the women, and hung down
or was turned back, according to the
freak of the wearer. Not only this,
but a new idea began, which was to
cut a hole in the long sleeve where
the hand came, and, pushing the
hand through, to let the rest of the
sleeve droop down. This developed,
as we shall see later.

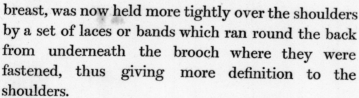

Then the cloak, which had before
been fastened by a brooch on the
shoulder or in the centre of the
breast, was now held more tightly over the shoulders
by a set of laces or bands which ran round the back
from underneath the brooch where they were
fastened, thus giving more definition to the
shoulders.

You must remember that such fashions as the
hole in the sleeve and the laced cloak were not any
more universal than is any modern fashion, and that

the good dame in the country was about a century behind the times with her loose gown and heavy cloak.

There were still the short gowns, which, being tucked in at the waist by the girdle, showed the thick wool chemise below and the unlaced gown, fitting like a jersey.

The large wimple was still worn wrapped about the head, and the hair was still carefully hidden.

Shall we imagine that it is night, and that the lady is going to bed? She is in her long white chemise, standing at the window looking down upon the market square of a small town.

The moon picks out every detail of carving on the church, and throws the porch into a dense gloom. Not a soul is about, not a light is to be seen, not a sound is to be heard.

The lady is about to leave the window, when she hears a sound in the street below. She peers down, and sees a man running towards the church; he goes in and out of the shadows. From her open window she can hear his heavy breathing. Now he darts into the shadow of the porch, and then out of the gloom comes a furious knocking, and a voice crying, ' Sanctuary !'

The lady at her window knows that cry well. Soon the monks in the belfry will awake and ring the Galilee-bell.

The Galilee-bell tolls, and the knocking ceases.

A few curious citizens look out. A dog barks. Then a door opens and closes with a bang.

There is silence in the square again, but the lady still stands at her window, and she follows the man in her thoughts.

Now he is admitted by the monks, and goes at once to the altar of the patron-saint of the church, where he kneels and asks for a coroner.

The coroner, an aged monk, comes to him and confesses him. He tells his crime, and renounces his rights in the kingdom ; and then, in that dark church, he strips to his shirt and offers his clothes to the sacrist for his fee. Ragged, mud-stained clothes, torn cloak, all fall from him in a heap upon the floor of the church.

Now the sacrist gives him a large cloak with a cross upon the shoulder, and, having fed him, gives him into the charge of the under-sheriff, who will

3—2

next day pass him from constable to constable towards the coast, where he will be seen on board a ship, and so pass away, an exile for ever.

The night is cold. The lady pulls a curtain across the window, and then, stripping herself of her chemise, she gets into bed.

HENRY THE FIRST

Reigned thirty-five years: 1100—1135.
Born 1068.   Married to Matilda of Scotland, 1100; to
Adela of Louvain, 1121.

THE MEN

THE Father of Popular Litera-
ture, Gerald of Wales, says:
'It is better to be dumb than
not to be understood. New
times require new fashions, and
so I have thrown utterly aside
the old and dry methods of
some authors, and aimed at
adopting the fashion of speech
which is actually in vogue
to-day.'

Vainly, perhaps, I have endeavoured to follow this pre-
cept laid down by Father Gerald, trying by slight
pictures of the times to make the dry bones live,

21

to make the clothes stir up and puff themselves into the shapes of men.

It is almost a necessity that one who would describe, paint, stage, or understand the costume of this reign should know the state of England at the time.

For there is in this reign a distinction without a difference in clothes; the shapes are almost identical to the shapes and patterns of the previous reigns, but everybody is a little better dressed.

The mantles worn by the few in the time of William the Red are worn now by most of the nobility, fur-lined and very full.

One may see on the sides of the west door of Rochester Cathedral Henry and his first wife, and notice that the mantle he wears is very full; one may see that he wears a supertunic, which is gathered round his waist. This tunic is the usual Norman tunic reaching to the knee, but now it is worn over an undertunic which reaches to the ground in heavy folds.

One may notice that the King's hair is long and elegantly twisted into pipes or ringlets, and that it hangs over his shoulders.

No longer is the priestly abuse of 'filthy goat'

A MAN OF THE TIME OF HENRY I.
(1100—1135)

His hair is curled in ringlets ; he wears a long cloak.
The shirt shows at the neck of the tunic. The small
design in the corner is from a sanctuary door-
knocker.

applicable, for Henry's beard is neatly trimmed and cut round his face.

These two things are the only practical difference between the two dates—the end of the eleventh century and the beginning of the twelfth.

The undertunic was made as a perfectly plain gown with tight sleeves ending at the wrist; it hung loose and full upon the figure. Over this was worn the short tunic with wide sleeves ending at the elbow. Both tunics would have broad borders of embroidered work or bands of coloured material. The supertunic would be brooched by one of those circular Norman brooches which was an ornamental circle of open goldwork in which stones and jewels were set. The brooch was fastened by a central pin.

The extravagances of the previous reign were in some measure done away with; even the very long hair was not fashionable in the latter half of this reign, and the ultra-long sleeve was not so usual.

So we may give as a list of clothes for men in this reign:

A white linen shirt.

A long tunic, open at the neck, falling to the ground, with tight sleeves to the wrist.

A short tunic reaching only to the knees, more open at the neck than the long tunic, generally fastened by a brooch.

Tight, well-fitting drawers or loose trousers.

Bandages or garters crossed from the ankle to the knee to confine the loose trousers or ornament the tights.

Boots of soft leather which had an ornamental band at the top.

Socks with an embroidered top.

Shoes of cloth and leather with an embroidered band down the centre and round the top.

Shoes of skin tied with leather thongs.

Caps of skin or cloth of a very plain shape and without a brim.

Belts of leather or cloth or silk.

Semicircular cloaks fastened as previously described, and often lined with fur.

The clothes of every colour, but with little or no pattern; the patterns principally confined to irregular groups of dots.

And to think that in the year in which Henry died Nizami visited the grave of Omar Al Khayyám in the Hira Cemetery at Nishapur !

THE WOMEN

The greatest change in the appearance of the women was in the arrangement of the hair.

After a hundred years or more of headcloths and hidden hair suddenly appears a head of hair. Until now a lady might have been bald for all the notice she took of her hair; now she must needs borrow hair to add to her own, so that her plaits shall be thick and long.

It is easy to see how this came about. The hair, for convenience, had always been plaited in two plaits and coiled round the head, where it lay concealed by the wimple. One day some fine lady decides to discard her close and uncomfortable head-covering. She lets her plaits hang over her shoulders, and so appears in public. Contempt of other ladies who have fine heads of hair for the thinness of her plaits; competition in thick and long hair; anger of ladies whose hair is not thick and long; enormous demand for artificial hair; failure of the supply to meet the ever-increasing demand; invention of silken cases filled with a substitute for hair, these cases attached to the end of the plaits to elongate them—in this manner do many fashions arrive and flourish, until such time as the common people find means of copying them, and then my lady wonders how she could ever have worn such a common affair.

The gowns of these ladies remained much the same, except that the loose gown, without any show of the figure, was in great favour; this gown was confined by a long girdle.

The girdle was a long rope of silk or wool, which was placed simply round the waist and loosely knotted; or it was wound round above the waist once, crossed behind, and then knotted in front, and the ends allowed to hang down. The ends of the girdle had tassels and knots depending from them.

The silk cases into which the hair was placed were often made of silk of variegated colours, and these cases had metal ends or tassels.

The girdles sometimes were broad bands of silk diapered with gold thread, of which manufacture specimens remain to us.

A WOMAN OF THE TIME OF HENRY I.
(1100—1135)

THIS shows the pendant sleeve with an embroidered hem. The long plaits of hair ended with metal, or silk, tags. At the neck and wrists the white chemise shows.

The sleeves of the gowns had now altered in shape, and had acquired a sort of pendulent cuff, which hung down about two hands' breadth from the wrist. The border was, as usual, richly ornamented.

Then we have a new invention, the pelisse. It is a loose silk coat, which is brooched at the waist, or buttoned into a silk loop. The sleeves are long—that is, they gradually increase in size from the underarm to the wrist, and sometimes are knotted at the ends, and so are unlike the other gown sleeves, which grow suddenly long near to the wrist.

This pelisse reaches to the knees, and is well open in front. The idea was evidently brought back from the East after the knights arrived back from the First Crusade, as it is in shape exactly like the coats worn by Persian ladies.

We may conceive a nice picture of Countess Constance, the wife of Hugh Lufus, Earl of

4—2

Chester, as she appeared in her dairy fresh from milking the cows, which were her pride. No doubt she did help to milk them; and in her long under-gown, with her plaits once more confined in the folds of her wimple, she made cheeses—such good cheeses that Anselm, Archbishop of Canterbury, rejoiced in a present of some of them.

What a change it must have been to Matilda, free of the veil that she hated, from the Black Nuns of Romsey, and the taunts and blows of her aunt Christina, to become the wife of King Henry, and to disport herself in fine garments and long plaited hair—Matilda the very royal, the daughter of a King, the sister to three Kings, the wife of a King, the mother of an Empress!

STEPHEN

Reigned nineteen years: 1135—1154.
Born 1094.   Married, 1124, to Matilda of Boulogne.

THE MEN

WHEN one regards the mass of material in existence showing costume of the tenth and eleventh centuries, it appears curious that so little fabric remains of this particular period.

The few pieces of fabric in existence are so worn and bare that they tell little, whereas pieces of earlier date of English or Norman material are perfect, although thin and delicate. There are few illuminated manuscripts of the twelfth century, or of the first half of it, and to the

29

few there are all previous historians of costume
have gone, so that one is left without choice but to
go also to these same books. The possibilities,
however, of the manuscripts referred to have not
been exhausted, and too much attention has been
paid to the queer drawing of the illuminators ; so
that where they utilized to the full the artistic
license, others have sought to pin it down as
accurate delineation of the costume of the time.
In this I have left out all the supereccentric
costumes, fearing that such existed merely in the
imagination of the artist, and I have applied myself to the more ordinary and understandable.
As there are such excellent works on armour, I
have not touched at all upon the subject, so that we
are left but the few simple garments that men wore
when they put off their armour, or that the peasant
and the merchant habitually wore.

Ladies occupied their leisure in embroidery and
other fine sewing, in consequence of which the
borders of tunics, of cloaks, the edgings of sleeves,
and bands upon the shoes, were elegantly patterned.
The more important the man, the finer his shoes.

As will be seen from the drawings, the man
wore his hair long, smoothly parted in the centre,

A MAN OF TH   STEPHEN

HE is wearing a cloak with hood attached; it is of
skin, the smooth leather inside. He has an ankle
gaiter covering the top of his shoes. On the arm
over which the cloak hangs can be seen the white
sleeve of the shirt.

with a lock drawn down the parting from the back of his head. As a rule, the hair curled back naturally, and hung on the shoulders, but sometimes the older fashion of the past reign remained, and the hair was carefully curled in locks and tied with coloured ribbon.

Besides the hood as covering for the head, men wore one or other of the simple caps shown, made of cloth or of fur, or of cloth fur-lined.

Next to his skin the man of every class wore a shirt of the pattern shown—the selfsame shirt that we wear to-day, excepting that the sleeves were made very long and tight-fitting, and were pushed back over the wrist, giving those wrinkles which we notice on all the Bayeux tapestry sleeves, and which we see for many centuries in drawings of the undergarment. The shape has always remained the same; the modes of fastening the shirt differ very slightly — so little, in fact, that a shirt of the fourth century which still remains in existence shows the same button and loop that we notice of the shirts of the twelfth century. The richer man had his shirt embroidered round the neck and sometimes at the cuffs. Over this garment the man wore

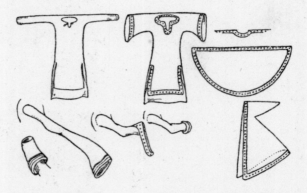

his tunic—of wool, or cloth, or (rarely) of silk ; the drawing explains the exact making of it. The tunic, as will be seen, was embroidered at the neck, the cuffs, and round the border. One drawing shows the most usual of these tunics, while the other drawings will explain the variations from it— either a tight sleeve made long and rolled back, a sleeve made very wide at the cuff and allowed to hang, or a sleeve made so that it fell some way over the hand. It was embroidered inside and out at the cuff, and was turned back to allow free use of the hand.

Over the tunic was worn the cloak, a very simple garment, being a piece of cloth cut in the shape of a semicircle, embroidered on the border or not, according to the purse and position of the owner. Sometimes a piece was cut out to fit the neck.

Another form of cloak was worn with a hood. This was generally used for travelling, or worn by such people as shepherds. It was made for the richer folk of fine cloth, fur-lined, or entirely of fur, and for the poorer people of skin or wool.

The cloak was fastened by a brooch, and was pinned in the centre or on either shoulder, most generally on the right ; or it was pushed through a ring sewn on to the right side of the neck of the cloak.

The brooches were practically the same as those worn in the earlier reigns, or were occasionally of a pure Roman design.

As will be seen in the small diagrams of men wearing the clothes of the day, the tunic, the shirt,

VOL. I.   5

and the cloak were worn according to the season, and many drawings in the MSS. of the date show men wearing the shirt alone.

On their legs men wore trousers of leather for riding, bound round with leather thongs, and trousers of wool also, bound with coloured straps of wool or cloth.

Stockings of wool were worn, and cloth stockings also, and socks. There was a sock without a foot, jewelled or em- broidered round the top, which was worn over the stocking and over the top of the boot in the manner of ankle gaiters.

The country man wore twists of straw round his calf and ankle.

For the feet there were several varieties of boots and shoes made of leather and stout cloth, now and again with wooden soles. As has been said before, the important people rejoiced in elegant footgear of all colours. All the shoes buttoned with one button above the outside ankle. The boots were sometimes tall, reaching to the bottom of the calf of the leg, and were rolled over, showing a coloured lining. Sometimes they were loose and wrinkled over the ankle. They were both, boot and shoe, made to fit the foot; for in this reign nearly all the extravagances of the previous reign had died out, and it is rare to find drawings or mention of long shoes stuffed with tow or wool.

During the reign of Stephen the nation was too occupied in wars and battles to indulge in excessive finery, and few arts flourished, although useful improvements occurred in the crafts.

There is in the British Museum a fine enamelled plate of this date which is a representation of Henry of Blois, Stephen's brother, who was the Bishop of Winchester. Part of the inscription, translated by Mr. Franks, says that 'Art is above gold and gems,' and that 'Henry, while living, gives gifts of brass to God.'

Champlevé enamel was very finely made in the twelfth century, and many beautiful examples remain, notably a plaque which was placed on the column at the foot of which Geoffrey Plantagenet was buried. It is a portrait of him, and shows the Byzantine influence still over the French style.

This may appear to be rather apart from costume, but it leads one to suppose that the ornaments of the time may have been frequently executed in enamel or in brass—such ornaments as rings and brooches.

It is hard to say anything definite about the colours of the dresses at this time. All that we can say is that the poorer classes were clothed principally in self-coloured garments, and that the dyes used for the clothes of the nobles were of very brilliant hues. But a street scene would be more occupied by the colour of armour. One would have seen a knight and men-at-arms—the knight in his plain armour and the men in leather and steel; a few merchants in coloured cloaks, and the common crowd in brownish-yellow clothes with occasional bands of colour encircling their waists.

The more simply the people are represented, the more truthful will be the picture or presentation. Few pictures of this exact time are painted, and few stories are written about it, but this will give all the information necessary to produce any picture or stage-play, or to illustrate any story.

The garments are perfectly easy to cut out and make. In order to prove this I have had them made from the bare outlines given here, without any trouble.

THE WOMEN

Though many parts of England were at this time being harassed by wars, still the domestic element grew and flourished.

The homes of the English from being bare and rude began to know the delights of embroidery and weaving. The workroom of the ladies was the most civilized part of the castle, and the effect of the Norman invasion of foreign fashions was beginning to be felt.

As the knights were away to their fighting, so were the knights' ladies engaged in sewing sleeve embroideries, placing of pearls upon shoes, making silk cases for their hair, and otherwise stitching, cutting, and contriving against the return of their lords.

It is recorded that Matilda escaped from Oxford by a postern in a white dress, and no doubt her women sympathizers made much of white for dresses.

The ladies wore a simple undergarment of thin material called a sherte or camise; this was bordered with some slight embroidery, and had tightish long sleeves pushed back over the wrist. The garment fell well on to the ground. This camise was worn by all classes.

The upper garment was one of three kinds: made from the neck to below the breast, including the sleeves of soft material; from the breast to the hips it was made of some elastic material, as knitted wool or thin cloth, stiffened by criss-cross bands of cloth, and was fitted to the figure and laced up the back; the lower part was made of the same material as the sleeves and bust.

The second was made tight-fitting in the body

A WOMAN OF THE TIME OF STEPHEN
(1135—1154)

HER dress fits to her figure by lacing at the back. Her long sleeves are tied up to keep them from trailing upon the ground. Her hair is fastened at the end into silken cases. She has a whimple in her hands which she may wind about her head.

A WOMAN OF THE TIME OF STEPHEN
(1135—1154)

HER dress fits to her figure by lacing at the back. Her long sleeves are tied up to keep them from trailing upon the ground. Her hair is fastened at the end into silken cases. She has a whimple in her hands which she may wind about her head.

A WOMAN OF THE TIME OF STEPHEN
(1135—1154)

HER dress fits to her figure by lacing at the back. Her long sleeves are tied up to keep them from trailing upon the ground. Her hair is fastened at the end into silken cases. She has a whimple in her hands which she may wind about her head.

and bust, all of one elastic material, and the skirt of loose thin stuff.

The third was a loose tunic reaching half-way between the knees and feet, showing the camise, and tied about the waist and hips by a long girdle.

The sleeves of these garments showed as many variations as those of the men, but with the poor folk they were short and useful, and with the rich they went to extreme length, and were often knotted to prevent them from trailing on the ground.

The collar and the borders of the sleeves were enriched with embroidery in simple designs.

In the case of the loose upper garment the border was also embroidered.

In winter a cloak of the same shape as was worn by the men was used—*i.e.*, cut exactly semicircular, with embroidered edges.

The shoes of the ladies were fitted to the foot in no extravagant shape, and were sewn with bands of pearls or embroidery. The poorer folk went about barefoot.

The hair was a matter of great moment and most carefully treated; it was parted in the centre and then plaited, sometimes intertwined with coloured ribbands or twists of thin coloured material; it was directed to building and the branches of architecture than to the more studious and sedentary works of illumination and writing, so that the sources from which we gather information with regard to the costume in England are few, and also peculiar, as the drawing of this date was, although careful, extremely archaic.

Picture the market-town on a market day when the serfs were waiting to buy at the stalls until the buyers from the abbey and the castle had had their pick of the fish and the meat. The lady's steward and the Father-Procurator bought carefully for their establishments, talking meanwhile of the annual catch of eels for the abbey.

Picture Robese, the mother of Thomas, the son of Gilbert Becket, weighing the boy Thomas each year on his birthday, and giving his weight in money, clothes, and provisions to the poor. She was a type of the devout housewife of her day, and the wife of a wealthy trader.

The barons were fortifying their castles, and the duties of their ladies were homely and domestic. They provided the food for men-at-arms, the followers, and for their husbands; saw that simples were ready with bandages against wounds and sickness; looked, no doubt, to provisions in case of siege; sewed with their maidens in a vestiary or workroom, and dressed as best they could for their position. What they must have heard and seen was enough to turn them from the altar of fashion to works of compassion. Their houses contained dreadful prisons and dungeons, where men were put upon rachentegs, and fastened to these beams so that they were unable to sit, lie, or sleep, but must starve. From their windows in the towers the ladies could see men dragged, prisoners, up to the castle walls, through the hall, up the staircase, and cast, perhaps past their very eyes, from the tower to the moat below. Such times and sights were not likely to foster proud millinery or dainty ways, despite of which innate vanity ran to ribbands in the hair, monstrous sleeves, jewelled shoes, and tight waists. The tiring women were not over-worked until a later period, when the hair would take hours to dress, and the dresses months to embroider.

In the town about the castle the merchants' wives wore simple homespun clothes of the same form as their ladies. The serfs wore plain smocks loose over the camise and tied about the waist, and

HENRY THE SECOND

Reigned thirty-five years: 1154—1189.
Born 1133.   Married, 1152, to Eleanor of Guienne.

THE MEN

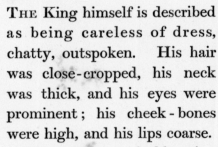

THE King himself is described as being careless of dress, chatty, outspoken.   His hair was close-cropped, his neck was thick, and his eyes were prominent; his cheek-bones were high, and his lips coarse.

The costume of this reign was very plain in design, but rich in stuffs.   Gilt spurs were attached to the boots by red leather straps, gloves were worn with jewels in the backs of them, and the mantles seem to have been ornamented with designs.

46

A MAN OF THE TIME OF HENRY II.
(1154—1189)

HE wears the short cloak, and his long tunic is held by a brooch at the neck and is girdled by a long-tongued belt.   There are gloves on his hands.

The time of patterns upon clothes began. The patterns were simple, as crescents, lozenges, stars.

William de Magna Villa had come back from the Holy Land with a new fabric, a precious silk called 'imperial,' which was made in a workshop patronized by the Byzantine Emperors.

The long tunic and the short supertunic were still worn, but these were not so frequently split up at the side.

High boots reaching to the calf of the leg were in common use.

That part of the hood which fell upon the shoulders was now cut in a neat pattern round the edge.

Silks, into which gold thread was sewn or woven, made fine clothes, and cloth cloaks lined with expensive furs, even to the cost of a thousand pounds of our money, were worn.

The loose trouser was going out altogether, and in its stead the hose were made to fit more closely to the leg, and were all of gay colours; they were gartered with gold bands crossed, the ends of which had tassels, which hung down when the garter was crossed and tied about the knee.

Henry, despite his own careless appearance, was

nicknamed Court Manteau, or Short Mantle, on account of a short cloak or mantle he is supposed to have brought into fashion.

The shirts of the men, which showed at the opening of the tunic, were buttoned with small gold buttons or studs of gold sewn into the linen.

The initial difference in this reign was the more usual occurrence of patterns in diaper upon the clothes.

The length of a yard was fixed by the length of the King's arm.

With the few exceptions mentioned, the costume is the same as in the time of Stephen.

It is curious to note what scraps of pleasant gossip come to us from these early times: St. Thomas à Becket dining off a pheasant the day before his martyrdom; the angry King calling to his knights, " How a fellow that hath eaten my bread, a beggar that first came to my Court on a lame horse, dares to insult his King and the Royal Family, and tread upon my whole kingdom, and not one of the cowards I nourish at my table, not one will deliver me of this turbulent priest !'—the veins no doubt swelling on his bull-like neck, the prominent eyes bloodshot with temper, the result of that angry speech, to end in the King's public penance before the martyr's tomb.

Picture the scene at Canterbury on August 23, 1179, when Louis VII., King of France, dressed in the manner and habit of a pilgrim, came to the shrine and offered there his cup of gold and a royal precious stone, and vowed a gift of a hundred hogsheads of wine as a yearly rental to the convent.

A common sight in London streets at this time was a tin medal of St. Thomas hung about the necks of the pilgrims.

And here I cannot help but give another picture. Henry II., passing through Wales on his way to Ireland in 1172, hears the exploits of King Arthur which are sung to him by the Welsh bards. In this song the bards mention the place of King Arthur's burial, at Glastonbury Abbey in the churchyard. When Henry comes back from Ireland he visits the Abbot of Glastonbury, and repeats to him the story of King Arthur's tomb.

One can picture the search: the King talking eagerly to the Abbot; the monks or lay-brothers digging in the place indicated by the words of the song; the knights in armour, their mantles wrapped about them, standing by.

VOL. I.   7

all a piece of fine linen is draped, and so arranged
that it shall just cover the forehead-band and fall
on to the shoulders. This last piece of linen is
fastened to the chin-band and the forehead-strap
by pins.

This fashion gave rise in later times to a linen
cap; the forehead-strap was increased in height and

stiffened so that it rose slightly
above the crown of the head,
and the wimple, instead of hanging over it, was sewn down inside
it, and fell over the top of the
cap. Later the cap was sewn
in pleats.

The gown of this time was
quite loose, with a deep band
round the neck and round the hem of the skirts,
which were very full. So far as one can tell, it
was put on over the head, having no other opening but at the neck, and was held at the waist
by an ornamental girdle.

The chemise showed above the neck of the gown,
which was fastened by the usual round brooch.

The sleeves were well fitting, rather loose at the
elbow, and fell shaped over the wrist, where there

A WOMAN OF THE TIME OF HENRY II.
(1154—1189)

THERE is a chin-band to be seen passing under the whimple; this band is pinned to hold it round the head.

was a deep border of embroidery. It is quite possible that the cuffs and hem may have been made of fur.

The shoes were, as usual to the last two reigns, rather blunt at the toe, and generally fitting without buckle, button, or strap round the ankle, where they were rolled back.

Above the waist the tied girdle was still worn, but this was being supplanted by a broad belt of silk or ornamented leather, which fastened by means of a buckle. The tongue of the belt was made very long, and when buckled hung down below the knee.

The cloaks, from the light way in which they are held, appear to have been made of silk or some such fine material as fine cloth. They are held on to the shoulders by a running band of stuff or a silk cord, the ends of which pass through two fasteners sewn on to the cloak, and these are knotted or have some projecting ornament which prevents the cord from slipping out of the fastener.

In this way one sees the cloak hanging from the shoulders behind, and the cord stretched tight across the breast, or the cord knotted in a second place, and so bringing the cloak more over the shoulders.

tible; if any difference may be noted, it is in the tinge of Orientalism in the garments.

There is more of the long and flowing robe, more of the capacious mantle, the wider sleeve.

No doubt the many who came from the Crusades made a good deal of difference to English homes, and actual dresses and tunics from the East, of gorgeous colours and Eastern designs, were, one must suppose, to be seen in England.

Cloth of gold and cloth of gold and silks—that is, warf of silk and weft of gold—were much prized, and were called by various names from the Persian, as 'ciclatoun,' 'siglaton.'

Such stuff, when of great thickness and value— so thick that six threads of silk or hemp were in the warf—was called 'samite.'

Later, when the cloth of gold was more in use, and the name had changed from 'ciclatoun' to 'bundekin,' and from that to 'tissue,' to keep such fine cloth from fraying or tarnishing, they put very thin sheets of paper away between the folds of the garments; so to this day we call such paper tissue-paper.

Leaf-gold was used sometimes over silk to give pattern and richness to it.

A MAN OF THE TIME OF RICHARD I.

(1189—1199)

A curious survival of this time, which has a connection with costume, was the case of Abraham Thornton in 1818. Abraham Thornton was accused of having drowned Mary Ashford, but he was acquitted by the jury. This acquittal did not satisfy popular feeling, and the brother of Mary Ashford appealed. Now Thornton was well advised as to his next proceeding, and, following the still existent law of this early time of which I write, he went to Westminster Hall, where he threw down, as a gage of battle, an antique gauntlet without fingers or thumb, of white tanned skin ornamented with silk fringes and sewn work, crossed by a narrow band of leather, the fastenings of leather tags and thongs.

This done, he declared himself ready to defend himself in a fight, and so to uphold his innocence, saying that he was within his rights, and that no judge could compel him to come before a jury.

This was held to be good and within the law, so Abraham Thornton won his case, as the brother refused to pick up the gauntlet. The scandal of this procedure caused the abolishment of the trial by battle, which had remained in the country's laws from the time of Henry II. until 1819.

the end ; the perfection of dress is to hide the milliner in the millinery.

The ladies of Richard I.'s time did not wear Oriental clothes, but they had a flavour of Orientalism pervading their dress—rather masculine Orientalism than feminine.

The long cloak with the cord that held it over the shoulders ; the long, loose gown of fine colours and simple designs ; the soft, low, heelless shoes ; the long, unbound hair, or the hair held up and concealed under an untied wimple—these gave a touch of something foreign to the dress.

Away in the country there was little to dress for, and what clothes they had were made in the house. Stuffs brought home from Cyprus, from Palestine, from Asia Minor, were laboriously conveyed to the house, and there made up into gowns. Local smiths and silver-workers made them buckles and brooches and ornamental studs for their long belts, or clasps for their purses.

A wreck would break up on the shore near by, and the news would arrive, perhaps, that some bales of stuff were washed ashore and were to be sold.

The female anchorites of these days were busy gossips, and from their hermitage or shelter by a

A WOMAN OF THE TIME OF RICHARD I.
(1189—1199)

HER very full cloak is kept in place by the cord which passes through loops. A large buckle holds the neck of the gown well together. The gown is ornamented with a simple diaper pattern; the hem and neck are deeply embroidered.

bridge on the road would see the world go by, and pick up friends by means of gifts of bandages or purses made by them, despite the fact that this traffic was forbidden to them.

So the lady in the country might get news of her lord abroad, and hear that certain silks and stuffs were on their way home.

The gowns they wore were long, flowing and loose; they were girded about the middle with leathern or silk belts, which drew the gown loosely together. The end of the belt, after being buckled, hung down to about the knee. These gowns were close at the neck, and there fastened by a brooch; the sleeves were wide until they came to the wrist, over which they fitted closely.

The cloaks were ample, and were held on by brooches or laces across the bosom.

The shoes were the shape of the foot, sewn, embroidered, elaborate.

The wimples were pieces of silk or white linen held to the hair in front by pins, and allowed to flow over the head at the back.

There were still remaining at this date women who wore the tight-fitting gown laced at the back, and who tied their chins up in gorgets.

JOHN

Reigned seventeen years : 1199—1216.
Born 1167. Married, in 1189, to Hadwisa, of Gloucester,
whom he divorced; married, in 1200, to Isabella
of Angoulême.

THE MEN

THERE was a garment in this reign which was the keynote of costume at the time, and this was the surcoat. It had been worn over the armour for some time, but in this reign it began to be an initial part of dress.

Take a piece of stuff about 9 or 10 yards in length and about 22 inches wide; cut a hole in the centre of this wide enough to admit of a man's head passing through, and you have a surcoat.

Under this garment the men wore a flowing gown, the sleeves of which were so wide that they

62

A MAN OF THE TIME OF JOHN
(1199—1216)

A MAN OF THE TIME OF JOHN
(1199—1216)

reached at the base from the shoulder to the waist, and narrowed off to a tight band at the wrist.

These two garments were held together by a leather belt buckled about the middle, with the tongue of the belt hanging down.

Broad borders of design edged the gowns at the foot and at the neck, and heraldic devices were sewn upon the surcoats.

King John himself, the quick, social, humorous man, dressed very finely. He loved the company of ladies and their love, but in spite of his love for them, he starved and tortured them, starved and beat children, was insolent, selfish, and wholly indifferent to the truth. He laughed aloud during the Mass, but for all that was superstitious to the degree of hanging relics about his neck; and he was buried in a monk's cowl, which was strapped under his chin.

Silk was becoming more common in England, and the cultivation of the silkworm was in some measure gaining hold. In 1213 the Abbot of Cirencester, Alexander of Neckham, wrote upon the habits of the silkworm.

Irish cloth of red colour was largely in favour, presumably for cloaks and hoods.

The general costume of this reign was very much the same as that of Henry II. and Richard I.—the long loose gown, the heavy cloak, the long hair cut at the neck, the fashion of beards, the shoes, belts, hoods, and heavy fur cloaks, all much the same as

before, the only real difference being in the general use of the surcoat and the very convenient looseness of the sleeves under the arms.

There is an inclination in writing of a costume one can visualize mentally to leave out much that might be useful to the student who knows little or nothing of the period of dress in which one is writing; so perhaps it will be better to now dress a man completely.

First, long hair and a neatly-trimmed beard; over this a hood and cape or a circular cap, with a slight projection on the top of it.

Second, a shirt of white, like a modern soft shirt.

Third, tights of cloth or wool.

Fourth, shoes strapped over the instep or tied

with thongs, or fitting at the ankle
like a slipper, or boots of soft leather
turned over a little at the top, at
the base of the calf of the leg.

Fifth, a gown, loosely fitting,
buckled at the neck, with sleeves
wide at the top and tight at the
wrist, or quite loose and coming to
just below the elbow, or a tunic
reaching only to the knees, both
gown and tunic fastened with a belt.

Sixth, a surcoat sometimes, at others a cloak held
together by a brooch, or made for travelling with a
hood.

This completes an ordinary wardrobe of the time.

THE WOMEN

As may be seen from the plate, no change in
costume took place.

The hair plaited and bound round the head or
allowed to flow loose upon the shoulders.

Over the hair a gorget binding up the neck and
chin.   Over all a wimple pinned to the gorget.

A long loose gown with brooch at the neck.

Sleeves tight at the wrist. The whole gown held in at the waist by a belt, with one long end hanging down.

Shoes made to fit the shape of the foot, and very elaborately embroidered and sewn.

A long cloak with buckle or lace fastening.

In this reign there were thirty English towns which had carried on a trade in dyed cloths for fifty years.

A WOMAN OF THE TIME OF JOHN
(1199—1216)

ONE may just see the purse beneath the cloak, where
it hangs from the belt. The cloak itself is of fine
diaper-patterned material.

HENRY THE THIRD

Reigned fifty-six years : 1216—1272.
Born 1207.   Married, 1236, to Eleanor of Provence.

THE MEN

DESPITE the fact that historians allude to the extravagance of this reign, there is little in the actual form of the costume to bear out the idea.   Extravagant it was in a large way, and costly for one who would appear well dressed ; but the fopperies lay more in the stuffs than in the cut of the garments worn.

It was an age of draperies.

This age must call up pictures of bewrapped people swathed in heavy cloaks of cloth of Flanders dyed with the famous Flemish madder dye ; of people in silk cloaks and gowns from Italy; of people in loose tunics made of English cloth.

9—2

This long reign of over fifty years is a transitional period in the history of clothes, as in its course the draped man developed very slowly towards the coated man, and the loose - hung clothes very gradually began to shape themselves to the body.

The transition from tunic and cloak and Oriental draperies is so slow and so little marked by definite change that to the ordinary observer the Edwardian cotehardie seems to have sprung from nowhere: man seems to have, on a sudden, dropped his stately wraps and mantles and discarded his chrysalis form to appear in tight lines following the figure—a form infinitely more gay and alluring to the eye than the ponderous figure that walks through the end of the thirteenth century.

Up to and through the time from the Conquest until the end of Henry III.'s reign the clothes of England appear—that is, they appear to me—to be lordly, rich, fine, but never courtier-like and elegant.

If one may take fashion as a person, one may say: Fashion arrived in 1066 in swaddling-clothes, and so remained enveloped in rich cloaks and flowing draperies until 1240, when the boy began to show a more active interest in life; this interest

A MAN OF THE TIME OF HENRY III.
(1216—1272)

HEAVY cloak and fulness of dress characteristic of
this time.

grew until, in 1270, it developed into a distaste for heavy clothes; but the boy knew of no way as yet in which to rid himself of the trailings of his mother cloak. Then, in about 1272, he invented a cloak more like a strange, long tunic, through which he might thrust his arms for freedom; on this cloak he caused his hood to be fastened, and so made himself three garments in one, and gave himself greater ease.

Then dawned the fourteenth century—the youth of clothes—and our fashion boy shot up, dropped his mantles and heaviness, and came out from thence slim and youthful in a cotehardie.

Of such a time as this it is not easy to say the right and helpful thing, because, given a flowing gown and a capacious mantle, imagination does the rest. Cut does not enter into the arena.

Imagine a stage picture of this time: a mass of wonderful, brilliant colours—a crowd of men in long, loose gowns or surcoats; a crowd of ladies in long, loose gowns; both men and women hung with cloaks or mantles of good stuffs and gay colours. A background of humbler persons in homespun tunics with cloth or frieze hoods over their heads. Here and there a fop—out of his date, a quarter-century before his time—in a loose coat with pocket-holes in front and a buttoned neck to his coat, his shoes very pointed and laced at the sides, his hair long, curled, and bound by a fillet or encompassed with a cap with an upturned brim.

The beginning of the coat was this: the surcoat, which up till now was split at both sides from the

shoulder to the hem, was now sewn up, leaving only a wide armhole from the base of the ribs to the shoulder. This surcoat was loose and easy, and was held in at the waist by a belt. In due time a surcoat appeared which was slightly shaped to the figure, was split up in front instead of at the sides, and in which the armholes were smaller and the neck tighter, and fastened by two or three buttons. In front of this surcoat two pocket-holes showed. This surcoat was also fastened by a belt at the waist.

In common with the general feeling towards more elaborate clothes, the shoes grew beyond their normal shape, and now, no longer conforming to the shape of the foot, they became elongated at the toes, and stuck out in a sharp point; this point was loose and soft, waiting for a future day when men should make it still longer and stuff it with tow and moss.

Of all the shapes of nature, no shape has been so marvellously maltreated as the human foot. It has suffered as no other portion of the body has suffered: it has endured exceeding length and exceeding narrowness; it has been swelled into broad, club-like shapes; it has been artificially raised from the ground, ended off square, pressed into tight points, curved under, and finally, as to-day, placed in hard, shining, tight leather boxes. All this has been done to one of the most beautiful parts of the human anatomy by the votaries of fashion, who have in turn been delighted to expose the curves of their bodies, the round swelling of their hips, the beauties of their nether limbs, the whiteness of their bosoms, the turn of their elbows and arms, and the rotundity of their shoulders, but who have, for some mysterious reasons, been for hundreds of years ashamed of the nakedness of their feet.

Let me give a wardrobe for a man of this time.

clothes. Paint the face, and you have a hint towards the condition of fashion.

Again, as in the case of the men, no determined cut shows which will point to this age as one of such and such a garment or such an innovation, but—and this I would leave to your imagination— there was a distinction that was not great enough to be a difference.

The gowns were loose and flowing, and were gathered in at the waist by a girdle, or, rather, a belt, the tongue of which hung down in front ; but as the end of the reign approached, the gowns were shaped a little more to the figure.

A lady might possess such clothes as these : the gowns I have mentioned above, the sleeves of which were tight all the way from the shoulder to the wrist, or were loose and cut short just below the elbow, showing the tight sleeves of the under-gown.

Shoes very elaborately embroidered and pointed at the toes.

A rich cloak made oblong in shape and very ample in cut.

A shaped mantle with strings to hold it together over the shoulders.

A WOMAN OF THE TIME OF HENRY III.
(1216—1272)

THIS will show how very slight were the changes in
woman's dress ; a plain cloak, a plain gown, and a
whimple over the head.

For the head a wimple made of white linen or perhaps of silk; this she would put above her head, leaving the neck bare.

A long belt for her waist, and, if she were a great lady, a pair of gloves to wear or stick into her belt.

10—2

THE COUNTRY FOLK

From the Conquest to the reign of Edward I.

UNTIL the present day the countryman has dressed in a manner most fitted to his surroundings; now the billycock hat, a devil-derived offspring from a Greek source, the Sunday suit of shiny black with purple trousers, the satin tie of Cambridge blue, and the stiff shirt, have almost robbed the peasant of his poetical appearance.

Civilization seems to have arrived at our villages with a pocketful of petty religious differences, a bagful of public-houses, a bundle of penny and halfpenny papers full of stories to show the fascination of crime, and—these Sunday clothes.

The week's workdays still show a sense of the
picturesque in corduroys and jerseys or blue shirts,
but the landscape is blotted with men wearing out
old Sunday clothes, so that the painter of rural
scenes with rural characters must either lie or
go abroad.

As for the countrywoman, she, I am thankful to
say, still retains a sense of duty and beauty, and,
except on Sunday, remains more or
less respectably clad. Chivalry prevents one from saying more.

In the old days—from the Conquest
until the end of the thirteenth century
—the peasant was dressed in perfect
clothes.

The villages were self-providing;
they grew by then wool and hemp
for the spindles. From this was made
yarn for materials to be made up into
coats and shirts. The homespun frieze that the
peasant wore upon his back was hung by the noble-
man upon his walls. The village bootmaker made,
besides skin sandals to be tied with thongs upon the
feet, leather trousers and belts.

The mole-catcher provided skin for hats. Hoods

of a plain shape were made from the hides of sheep
or wolves, the wool or hair being left on the hood.
Cloaks lined with sheepskin served to keep away
the winter cold.

To protect their legs from thorns the men wore
bandages of twisted straw wrapped round their
trousers, or leather thongs cross-gartered to the
knee.

The fleece of the sheep was woven in the summer
into clothes of wool for the winter. Gloves were
made, at the beginning of the thirteenth century,
of wool and soft leather; these were shaped like the
modern baby's glove, a pouch for the hand and
fingers and a place for the thumb.

A coarse shirt was worn, over which a tunic, very
loosely made, was placed, and belted at the waist.
The tunic hardly varied in shape from the Conquest
to the time of Elizabeth, being but a sack-like
garment with wide sleeves reaching a little below
the elbow. The hood was ample and the cloak
wide.

The women wore gowns of a like material to the
men—loose gowns which reached to the ankles and
gave scope for easy movement. They wore their
hair tied up in a wimple of coarse linen.

A PEASANT OF EARLY ENGLAND
(William I.—Henry III.)

His hood is made from sheep-skin, the wool outside, the hem trimmed into points. His legs are bound up with garters of plaited straw. His shoes are of the roughest make of coarse leather. He has the shepherd's horn slung over his shoulder.

The people of the North were more ruggedly clothed than the Southerners, and until the monks founded the sheep-farming industry in Yorkshire the people of those parts had no doubt to depend for their supply of wool upon the more cultivated peoples.

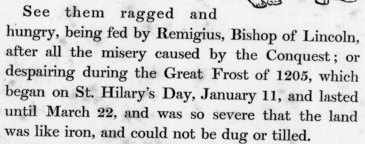

Picture these people, then, in very simple natural wool-coloured dresses going about their ordinary country life, attending their bees, their pigs, sheep, and cattle, eating their kele soup, made of cole-wort and other herbs.

See them ragged and hungry, being fed by Remigius, Bishop of Lincoln, after all the misery caused by the Conquest; or despairing during the Great Frost of 1205, which began on St. Hilary's Day, January 11, and lasted until March 22, and was so severe that the land was like iron, and could not be dug or tilled.

When better days arrived, and farming was taken more seriously by the great lords, when Grosseteste, the Bishop of Lincoln, wrote his book on farming and estate management for Margaret, the Dowager-

Countess of Lincoln, then clothes and stuffs manu-factured in the towns became cheaper and more easy to obtain, and the very rough skin clothes and undressed hides began to vanish from among the clothes of the country, and the rough gartered trouser gave way before cloth cut to fit the leg.

On lord and peasant alike the sun of this early age sets, and with the sunset comes the warning bell—the *couvre-feu*—so, on their beds of straw-covered floors, let them sleep. . . .

END OF VOL. I